m o m

jacquelyn lee

mind over mother

ISBN: 9781082279485

Printed in the United States of America.

Written, edited, designed and self-published by Jacquelyn Lee.

Also by Jacquelyn Lee

under the influence

to every child
who had to grow up
motherless
this is for you

i wrote this with you in mind
the one who grew up thinking
you were alone

the one who grew up thinking
you were the only one

i am here to tell you that
you were never alone
you were never the only one

while i was growing up motherless
i had no one to relate to
i had no one in the same situation as me
or so i thought

i felt so misunderstood
i felt so lost

there are so many of us
growing up this way
yet we don't even realize it

it is time that we talk about our trauma
it is time that we join together
it is time that we help each other heal

to the one who
grew up motherless
– this is for you

I am not writing this book
because I want to
I am writing this book
because I must

to my younger siblings
paul jr.
larissa
and justin
i'm sorry for the pain
our mother caused you

to my aunt neen
thank you for always
being a second mother to us since birth

to my grandma
thank you for always
being there for us since birth

trigger warning . . .

this book contains
highly sensitive content
related to...

abuse
abandonment
agoraphobia
alcoholism
anxiety
childhood trauma
death
delusions
depression
domestic violence
drug addiction
eating disorders
family dysfunction
grief
hallucinations
mental illness
menstruation
self-harm
sexual abuse
suicide

& more

please don't forget to practice self-love
while reading and always

xoxo

preface . . .

after eight long years of ignoring the question,
"but, where is your mom?"
it feels so liberating to finally answer it.

no, my mother is not a drug addict.
no, she didn't die.
she is mentally ill—
and she refuses to admit it.

so it eats away at her soul every day.

her mind has convinced itself
that it isn't the *right time* for her to be with her kids.
or, in her words, *"God"* told her that.

but, it hasn't been the *right time* for
eight.
long.
years.

you would think i hate my mother.
but i don't.
you would think i resent my mother.
but i don't. *anymore.*

i have grown to feel sorry for her.
i have grown to understand her.

she lives mentally imprisoned.
she can't escape the thoughts in her mind.

my only hope is that one day,
she can heal all of her pain.

contents

chapter one
the breakdown

This is not a story of abuse.
This is a story of *abandonment.*

This is not a story of drug use.
This is a story of *mental illness.*

My parents are two very different people
who hurt me in two very different ways.

You read one part of the story,
now, here are the missing pieces.

Here is what growing up without a mother was like.

open letter number one

Mom,

My intention is not to call you out for abandoning us.
I do not hate you. I am not mad at you.

I intend to show the world
how to forgive a parent who left,
how to heal from it,
and how to move on in life.

I intend to shed light on mental illness,
and to give families affected by it a sense of comfort
with every word written in this book.

I forgive you.
I understand your illness.
And my only hope is for you to get better.

This book is so hard to write
and I don't know why.

Maybe it's because
my father was dead when I wrote about him
and my mother is still alive while I'm writing about her.

Or maybe it's because
writing about my mother is forcing me to express
all of my repressed feelings from the age of thirteen.

Or maybe it's because
publishing a book about
growing up motherless makes it real.

Or maybe it's
all of the above.

I don't know if it's hard to write about you because I am
Emotionless about you
or because I have too many emotions about you.

my mother
is afraid of life.

she was diagnosed
with agoraphobia years ago.

basically, that means
she is afraid of
going out in the world.

she has severe anxiety
in public and social settings.

she's afraid to
drive a car,
go out in public,
and
so much more.

even when
she did drive,
she never drove outside of our hometown.

even when
she did go out,
she never went to unknown places.

she was able to survive like this for a while.

but over time,
her condition worsened.

she went from only driving around our hometown,
to not driving at all.

she went from only going to familiar places,
to not going anywhere at all.

then, she stopped working.
and she barely left the couch.

she couldn't even
walk down the block to
get her children
to and from the bus stop
every day.

after a little while,
she got somewhat better.

even though she didn't live with us,
and even though she was still delusional,
she would come pick us up from our dad's house
in the morning to drive us to school.

and then,
she would pick us up from school in the afternoon.
i used to walk to the starbucks
that was near my high school
to get coffee after my last class ended.
so, she would pick me up from there.

and for some reason, every single day,
she would *spill* water on the passenger seat.
she would tell me *"don't sit in the front, i spilled water there,"*
and i would get into the backseat of the car with my coffee.
this became an odd routine.

i never asked her *why* she did this. and i probably never will.

was she afraid that something would happen to me if i sat in the
passenger seat? was this a part of her religious delusion, some
kind of ritual? or, did she just not want me to sit next to her?

- i don't think i'll ever find out *why.*

i am allowed to understand my mother's illness
and also feel hurt by her

i am allowed to understand why my mother left us
and also feel betrayed by her

i am allowed to feel hurt by my mother
and still love her

i am allowed to feel betrayed by my mother
and still care about her

mental illness
does not simply happen
because of your genetics

there is no depression gene
there is no anxiety gene
there is no bipolar gene
there is no schizophrenia gene

mental illness
runs in families
because trauma
runs in families

mental illness
runs in families
because dysfunction
runs in families

mental illness
runs in families
because abuse
runs in families

be the one
to break the cycle
in your family

generational curses
end with *y o u.*

my father was the DJ at my mother's sweet sixteen
ever since they met that day, he swept her off her feet

she was only sixteen
and
he was only eighteen

they fell in love and got married
way too young, way too fast

my mother graduated high school
and immediately married my father
she was only eighteen, and he was only twenty

my mother didn't ever have a chance to live,
she didn't ever have a chance to find herself

she had me at nineteen, and then my brother
and then my sister, and then my youngest brother

her whole life was being a mom,
and from what i heard, she did a good job

flash forward to this year,
and she is not here

the girl who had no aspirations in life

other than being a mom

gave
     up
         on
             her
                 children

i have vivid memories
of being around eight-years-old
telling my mom that she should
go to college
telling my mom that she should
pursue a career

i was only eight-years-old
and i sensed
the emptiness in my mother's life

i have vivid memories
of my mother at the kitchen table
writing in notebooks while drinking coffee
i remember her reading what she wrote to me

she wanted to write books
she wanted to pursue something

and i wish that she would have
i really, really wish that she would have

if so, i wouldn't have to be writing this book

dysfunction attracts dysfunction

both of my parents
came from dysfunction

i know that's why
they once found comfort in each other

the problem is
it's only a matter of time
before that dysfunction leads to destruction

if only my poor mother would've known
what was in store

if only my poor mother would've known
what was knocking at her door

if only my poor mother would've known
to walk away

if only she knew,
it would've saved her yesterdays

What I didn't know then, and what I clearly know now
is how much dad abused you.

What I didn't know then, and what I clearly know now
is why you took your wedding ring off.

If I knew then, what I know now
I would've told you how strong you were.

I'm so sorry for what you went through, Mom.
I'm so sorry that I didn't know.

list of things number one

things my mom claimed that God told her:

1. that a man would come to our house in a mercedes-benz, and ask her to marry him

2. that a woman would message her on facebook, and give her a business to take over

3. that she should quit her job

4. that she couldn't be with her kids anymore

5. that my husband was already chosen for me (i was 12.)

6. that our family would be restored, and her and my father would remarry (they tried. it didn't work out.)

7. that she and i would write a book together (ironic, because i wrote a book about her instead.)

8. that my siblings and i had to go through what we went through in order to learn disappointment

list of things number two

things my mom claimed that God told her, that actually happened:

I was never able to look up to my mother
as a strong, independent woman.

But somehow, I still turned out to be
a strong, independent woman.

I didn't have a role model growing up.
I had to become my own role model.
Way too soon, way too young.

I had to look in the mirror and tell myself,
"this is not what I want for my future."

I had to examine my mother's life:
she was in her thirties,
divorced from a toxic man,
living in tiny apartments with four kids,
cleaning houses for a living,
barely making ends meet,
depressed and stressed out all of the time.

Back then, I thought,
*"I want my life to be better than hers.
I want my life to be full."*

Now, as I've grown up,
I realize how much my mother tried back then.
She *really* tried.
She did the single mom thing.
She took care of us as best as she could.

But her mental illness was always lingering.
We couldn't see it, but it was always there.

Depression got the best of her.
It stole her kids.
It stole her life.
It stole her ability to steal back what belongs to her.

With a tap on the shoulder,
I heard a soft voice whisper my name,
"Jacquelyn."

I turned around and uttered,
"Um, hi. D-do I know you?"

"No, darling, I'm afraid you don't yet know who I am,"
said the soft-voiced woman, *"But, I surely know you."*

She didn't look of this world. Her pale skin glowed and her green eyes beamed in the sunlight. Her rosy red lips spoke only gentle words. She carried a light within her. Something about her made me feel whole. I don't know what it was. But, looking at her made me feel as though I was looking at my reflection in the mirror. It was an out-of-body experience.

"W-what do you mean?" I replied.

*"Save your questions, sweetie.
I've come to prepare you for what's to come."*

*"Huh? Listen, I'm not supposed to talk to strangers.
I'm only seven, you know."*

"Only seven you are, my dear. You see, one day you're going to look back and remember the days when you were only seven. One day, you're going to look back and wonder where the time has gone. This will be long after your mother has a mental breakdown six years from now."

"What? My mom? H-how do you know that's going to happen?"

"Don't worry, honey. Don't you worry. Everything is going to be okay. But, let me tell you, your life is going to be one hell of a roller coaster ride."

28

"I've never been on a roller coaster before."

"I know, I know. You're afraid of heights.
But that's going to change.
After the life you live,
you will fear everything and nothing all at once."

"I'm not really sure what you mean, but, okay."

- the beginning of another book that i may never finish.

advice for young writers

Write as much as you breathe. Bring a notepad everywhere you go. Just write.

Write down every idea that you get. If you don't, you will forget it. I promise you that.

Read. A lot. The best inspiration comes from reading books.

Don't be afraid to hurt anyone's feelings when you write. You wouldn't have to write about them if they didn't hurt you in the first place.

Be brutally honest. Be raw. Be bold.
And most importantly, be yourself.

Don't compare yourself to other writers. Period.

It doesn't matter how many followers your writing accounts have. It doesn't matter how many likes you get on your posts. Just keep writing.

Everyone's story is different. Don't be discouraged if you don't grow faster than someone else. Your time will come.

Educate yourself. Read books. Research different topics. Watch documentaries. Pick the brains of your relatives. Learning more will only make your writing better.

Your writing is not going to be everyone's cup of tea. Do not be moved by negative opinions. Nothing of quality ever goes without being criticized.

You should only worry when *everyone* likes your writing.

i've been snoozing the alarm
on writing this book.

every.
single.
morning.

i want to write this book,
but it's so hard to think about
these old memories.

it's so hard to
face the fact
that this is reality.

it's so hard to
let these feelings out.

but it's a step i need to take.

i need to express and
release these emotions
so i can heal this pain.

- if you've been snoozing the alarm on writing your own book,
here is your wake up call.

Mom,

The difference between you and Dad is that
you never did anything to hurt us intentionally

The pain you've caused was never on purpose
you hurt us without realizing you were doing a damn thing

Yeah, Dad slapped me across the face with his bare hands
it hurt for a while,
but it doesn't anymore

Yeah, Dad stole thousands of dollars from me
my bank account was negative for a while,
but it isn't anymore

The pain of knowing that my mother is out there in this world,
and hasn't made an effort to see my face in two years, is *constant*

The pain of knowing you think that this is all God,
when it isn't at all, is *constant*

Even if I seem okay
even if I am not thinking about it
it's a pain that will always be there subconsciously

open letter number three

Mom,

I watched you smoke your lungs black
trying to escape the darkness that was your life

I watched you as your teeth and fingernails yellowed,
and your face began to age

I watched you as you blacked out while driving
with all four of your kids in the car
from smoking too many cigarettes on an empty stomach

I watched you as you slept on the couch
and had trouble breathing at night

I watched you as your health deteriorated
and your addiction took over

You and Dad were alike but similar,
your addictive personalities were one and the same

You just chose two different vices,
trying to take your pain away

open letter number four

Mom,

I don't know if you ever realized but,
Paulie and I used to
steal some of your cigarettes,
crush them up,
and throw them in the trash

We knew we'd get caught if we threw away the entire pack,
but we figured it would be a little bit better
if there were less cancer sticks for you to smoke

I was only eleven and
he was seven-years-old

We shouldn't have even known about cigarettes at those ages,
the least you could've done was hide your dirty habit

Eventually, you kicked it and you quit cold turkey
and I'm proud of you for that

Your smoking was one less thing I had to
worry about at eleven-years-old

If only I knew then about all the worries
the absence of you would bring me

open letter number five

Mom,

I never really told anyone this but,
when I was in high school and life got stressful,
I started smoking cigarettes, just like you

I always wondered what they did for you,
and why you smoked them,
so I justified my smoking by thinking
well, my mom always did it
even though I knew it was a horrible habit to have

I didn't do it excessively,
just during the really rough times
after a while, I stopped caring for it
I don't do it anymore
and I probably never will again

I made a promise to myself to be as least like you as possible

Because
I am not you
I am not you
I am not you

my google search history when i was thirteen:

what is a "religious yoke"

my mom thinks God talks to her

religious delusion

my mom says God told her to quit her job

what is schizophrenia?

is God real?

open letter number six

Mom,

Why did this happen?
Is it because the church brainwashed you?
Is it because of what Dad put you through?
Is it because you stopped taking your antidepressants?

There are so many questions I have for you,
But this is one that I feel like I'll never get an answer to.

Why? Why did this happen to you?

list of things number three

things that led to my mother's breakdown:

1. prolonged, undiagnosed mental illness

2. the fact that mental illnesses used to be taboo

3. possible sexual assault

4. an abusive marriage

5. undiagnosed postpartum depression

6. having kids and getting married too young

7. terrible advice from a so-called church counselor

8. terrible advice from so-called friends of hers

9. refusing to take her antidepressants

10. refusing to seek psychiatric help

Both of my parents have made claims
that they were sexually abused.

I know that some people might say
that they aren't the most credible sources.
I know that most people wouldn't believe them.
My father was constantly drunk and high.
My mother constantly has delusions and hallucinations.

Obviously they can both be making up stories, right?
Yes, it is likely that their claims may not be true.
But, it is also just as likely that their claims are very true.
It is also just as likely that their claims are what caused them
to get drunk,
to get high,
to have delusions,
to have hallucinations.

At this point, we can never know for sure
what happened to them.
But, in my heart, I choose to believe them.
Because we can never know.
And it isn't up to me or anyone else to invalidate their stories.

My parents weren't messed up for no reason.
I don't know who,
I don't know what,
I don't know where,
and I don't know when.

But in my heart,
I know that something bad
happened to both of them.

I cannot write this book without acknowledging something very crucial that happened to my mother. While this was happening, I was only thirteen. I was aware of what was going on, but I was just a kid. I am twenty-one-years-old now, I've experienced a lot more in life and I have a much deeper understanding of what happened to my mother.

I'm going to preface this by saying that this is the version of the story that I remember. This is written from my own perspective at thirteen-years-old as my mother's daughter. With that being said, let's get into the story.

I'm just going to say it flat out: the church played a huge role in my mother's breakdown.

Yes. The church.

I'm not going to name this church, but I am going to talk about what happened here and how corrupt the individuals involved truly are.

I guess I should start by saying that I was sort of raised as a Christian by my mother. I say *"sort of"* because I have no memory of her teaching me anything about Christianity, honestly. She never taught me much about The Bible, God, how to be a "good" Christian, or the meaning behind anything in Christianity. (I'm not sure about my siblings, again, this is how I remember my childhood.) All I remember my mother doing when it comes to being raised as a Christian, is dragging me to church every Sunday morning. I honestly just sat there, not really understanding much about anything. I knew the popular Bible stories, like Adam and Eve and Noah's Ark, but who doesn't know about those?

Anyway, the point here is that I don't feel like I was raised as a Christian by my mother, because she never really instilled much about the religion in me. It's actually sort of humorous to think about and also very hypocritical of her, since she claims to be such a devout Christian woman.

So, that was my childhood for a while. Being dragged to church on Sunday, but never being taught much about the belief system. I think the reason why this happened is because this church was really more like a cult. I vividly remember going to a youth group one Friday night and having someone a bit older than me ask me what kind of music I like. After I told her the kind of music I liked to listen to, she started telling me about different types of Christian music in an attempt to make me change the music I listen to. Like, what even?! Looking back on this memory, it really just makes me realize how insane this specific church is. *God forbid anyone listens to the type of music they enjoy.*

But, let's get into the story of how the church played such a huge role in my mother's breakdown.

My mother was having extreme delusions, thinking that God was telling her things like: "quit your job," "a man is going to come to your house in a brand new Mercedes and become your new husband," "a woman is going to call you and give you a business." Now, you would think that if anyone had these insane delusions and actually thought God was speaking to them, the church would advise them to get psychiatric help immediately.

But no, f*ck psychology, right?

This church actually confirmed that these thoughts were coming from God himself, and encouraged my mom to believe these delusions. Well, it's been eight years. *"God's plan"* for my mother's life still hasn't happened. I'd love to know what the people from this church have to say about this entire situation now.

Maybe I shouldn't blame the entire church, because it was one specific *"church counselor"* or whoever that was encouraging my mother to listen to her delusions. But, there was an entire congregation of people who saw this going on and did absolutely nothing to stop it. So, yeah, I'm going to blame this entire church.

These unqualified *"church counselors"* who know nothing about psychology and counseling yet believe they are *"called by God"* to counsel others are extremely problematic. Nobody should have been encouraging my mother to quit life. Nobody should have been telling my mother it was God's voice telling her to stop being an adult. And most importantly, nobody should have been telling my mother it was God's voice telling her to stop being a mother.

My mother was, sadly, brainwashed by this church to begin with. I think the delusions began somewhere after the brainwashing. Then, this so-called counselor encouraged her to believe the delusions, so that this would further enforce the brainwashing. Eight years later, she is still brainwashed and waiting for her *"breakthrough."*

How was she brainwashed, you wonder? Well, they preach the idea that *the more money you give to them, the more money God will bless you with*. So, there were times that my mother literally gave this church the food out of our mouths.

I'm not saying that all churches are bad.
I'm just saying that *this one* is.

So, yeah.

This was my most vivid experience with the Christian church.

That is all.

some people
are greatly
helped by their churches.

i understand that.

but so many others
are deeply
hurt by their churches.

my mother was
one of those people.

so, please understand
my reason for telling this story.

my mother was
hurt so badly
by these people.

her life was destroyed.

and
i am done
staying silent
about it.

- to those of you who hurt her: ***shame on you.***

"so, your mother is a narcissist?"

no, not at all.

"so, your mother is crazy?"

no, not at all.

"so, she must be a terrible mother?"

no, not at all.

my mother is not a narcissist.
my mother is not crazy.
my mother is not a terrible mother.

my mother is a victim.
my mother is sick.
my mother is traumatized from years of abuse.

she is unable to care for her kids.
she did not willingly leave us.
she was left with no choice.

      she is too torn down to get back on her own two feet.

one day.
maybe one day.
she will be okay.

      but, by the time that day comes.
        it may be too late.

give us all of your love
or give us
nothing at all, mom

- this seemed like the right thing to say then, i now realize it wasn't

be a full-time mom
or don't be
a mom at all
they say

why is it seen as commonplace
for a father
to be around part-time

but when a mother
is around part-time
it is seen as out of this world?

why is being a single mom
seen as strong, as independent

while being a single dad
is seen as sad
as something that shouldn't happen

why are single moms
so normalized

but when things are the other
way around,
it is seen as so atypical?

- *normalize single dads, too.*

"give the kids
your all
or give them
nothing.

they deserve the whole cake,
they don't deserve *crumbs.* "

- something my father used to tell my mother

all or nothing

the problem with asking someone with a mental illness
to give you their all or nothing
is that they can't possibly give you their all

they are incapable of giving you
more than they can handle

so, if you ask them to give you
their all or nothing

they will give you

nothing

you messed me up
in so many ways

so much so that
i don't dream of
having a wedding day

<u>two different sisters</u>

how can the same mother create two different sisters?

she already has her baby names picked out
while i have no clue

she has always known she wants to be a mother one day
while i am still not sure

she dreams of having the perfect wedding day
while i have no desire for one

are we two different sisters?
or am i just messed up?

are we two different sisters?
or am i the only girl in the world who feels this way?

I know that I keep saying this, but,
this book is so hard to write

Because I'm not writing about you
I'm writing about the *absence of you*

How do you write about someone who you don't even know?
How do you write about someone who isn't around?

How do you write about someone who is so
out of sight, out of mind?

out of sight, out of mind

that's what dad used to tell us
when we didn't see you, we didn't think of you
and it was true.

as i'm writing this, i haven't seen you in
five-hundred and fifty-five days.

that's one year,
six months,
and eight days,
to be more clear.

that's thirteen thousand three hundred and twenty
hours of my life that you've missed.

that's seven hundred ninety-nine thousand and two hundred
motherless minutes that i've lived.

that's forty-seven million nine hundred and fifty-two thousand
seconds that have passed by without your presence.

that's out of sight, out of mind.

- *it's been over two years now.*

"Your mother used to write your name,
J a c q u e l y n
all over her notebooks when she was in high school.
She had your name picked out long before you were born."

Many people have told me this.
"All she ever wanted to do was have kids,"
so they say.

My mother picked out my name
when she was in high school,
And yet she abandoned me
when I was in high school.

My mother wanted nothing more than to be a mother
when she was in high school,
And yet I had to take on her role as a mother
when I was in high school.

- Is this ironic, or is it just sad? I can't tell.

You may have given me my name,
but you don't get credit for my strength.
You are not responsible for my resilience.

What you put me through did not make me stronger,
no,
I was already strong.

chapter two
the breakaway

"its not like you guys are bad kids. that would somewhat explain why she left you guys. but, you guys are good kids. you guys are good kids and she's missing out on your lives."

- something our father would say to us often

who is the lesser of two evils?

a mother who wasn't there for us, but never abused us,
or a father who was there for us, but wound up abusing us?

Mom,

you left dad because he abused you
you left dad because you were in danger

i didn't realize it then,
i was only seven
but i know it now

you left dad because
he picked me up and shook me
in anger

you left dad because
of all the glass plates
he threw at the walls

you left dad because
he cheated on you

you left dad because
he didn't treat you right

and then,
when it came time for us
to move in with him

you said it was God
you said it was what we needed

but, mom, what did you think was going to happen?

i know that people *can* change

i know it seemed like dad *did* change

and, at first he was okay
but, he only got worse
over the years

you left dad because he shook me

and i left dad because he hit me

you left dad because he abused you

and i left dad because he abused me

what did you think was going to happen?
did you really foresee a happy ending?

none of this would've ever happened
none of this should've ever happened

things were *not* ever supposed to be this way
this was never God
this was never what we needed

- we needed our mom.

open letter number eight

Mom,

I don't remember everything exactly
I don't remember every single time you left,
and every single time that you came back around

But what I do remember is that you were inconsistent
you were around one day
and you were gone the next

And it really doesn't matter if you left because
you were afraid of dad,
or because
you really believed that God told you to leave

All that matters is that
nothing in the world is natural about
a mother abandoning their children

on my eighteenth birthday
i got my first tattoo

my mother stopped by that day
like she often did on special occasions

she told me that
having a tattoo on my upper back
won't look too good on my wedding day

she told me that
i'll have to find a dress
to cover it up

my mother was worried about what i'll look like
on my wedding day

yet she doesn't even see what i look like
on a daily basis

my mother was worried about
me getting married

yet she has never met one of my
significant others

my mother was worried about finding me
a wedding dress

yet i can't remember the last time she came shopping
for clothing with me

- *maybe this is why i hate the idea of having a wedding.*

list of things number four

things you don't know as a female growing up without a mother:

1. what a period is

2. how to use a tampon

3. when you should start seeing an ob-gyn

4. what's normal and not normal when it comes to your period

5. anything about female anatomy, basically

6. how to swallow a pill

7. how to make a french braid in your hair

(i also never learned how to ride a bike, does that one count too?)

I got my first period
and I had
no idea what it was

I had no idea
what was happening
to me

I came home in tears
I thought something
was seriously
wrong with me

I was so young
I was so afraid

My mother didn't
teach me anything
about being a female

She didn't prepare me for life

She wasn't there
when I was sixteen
and almost passed out
in school
from the pain
of having ovarian cysts

I needed my mom
I needed her to be there for me
I needed her to guide me

And she wasn't there

to the motherless on mothers day
written on mother's day 2018

growing up without a mother is like driving to an unknown location without a map in front of you. you can still make it there somehow, but you lack direction. you can only understand this if you've experienced it for yourself.

if merely seeing the word *"motherless"* gives you chills, then, you know what it feels like to mourn a mother and be labeled: motherless.

so, here's to the motherless on mother's day. i wrote this for you. to let you know that you are not alone. that you aren't the only one who had to grow up fending for yourself. our stories may differ in many ways, but trust me-- on this day and every day, we remain one and the same.

i spent years avoiding social media on this day. because it made me sick to see a timeline full of photos of everyone else with their mothers, while mine was nowhere to be found.

she lets months pass by without calling her children let alone seeing us. and then she expects to be acknowledged on mother's day each year. as if she deserves a card and a bouquet of flowers after doing nothing for us but cause us pain.

for a very long time, this day has been a day full of confusion, resentment and anger for my siblings and me. and i know that we aren't the only ones who feel this way. who feel abandoned. who feel unwanted. who feel rejected.

the only thing worse than mourning a mother who has died is having no choice but to mourn one who is still alive. *not only is this uneasy to explain, but it is extremely difficult for others to understand.*

when your teachers in school tell you to *"make sure you ask your mom to sign this,"* you just smile and nod. because it's too hard to explain to them that your mother is alive, but you never see her.

the women your father date take the anger they have towards your mother out on you, *"why don't you ask your mother to do that for you?"* and *"why am i stuck doing your mother's job?"* is what you hear from them. as if it was your fault that she lost her mind.

your friend's parents make comments like, *"how can a mother just abandon her children?!"* and *"if she ever decides to come back into your life, she isn't even going to remember how to be a mother."* although you know it's true, it still hurts to hear it.

in sharing my story with the world, i have learned that knowing there are others in the world who you can relate to is one of the most comforting feelings.

so, if you can relate to these words in one way or another, please know that i wrote this for you. you are close to my heart always and on my mind a little bit extra today. i feel the pain that you feel. i've felt every ounce of resentment that you feel. *you are not alone.*

do not beat yourself up over your mother's mistakes. her mistakes do not define you. you are not your mother. you are not her mistakes. and most importantly: *you will be okay.*

here's to the motherless on mother's day.
here's to the orphans wondering why their mothers didn't want them a little bit extra today.
here's to the kids who have been in and out of foster homes their entire life, wondering what stability feels like.
here's to the kids who watched their mother take her last breath.
here's to the kids who were abandoned by their mothers, whether the reason is drugs, alcoholism, mental illness, or selfishness.
here's to the kids who live with their abusive mothers.
here's to the kids who have mothers who do nothing but point out

their flaws and talk down to them every day instead of building them up.

and lastly, here's to the women who have picked up the slack and made a difference in the lives of children who have been neglected and abandoned by the person who brought them into this world.

here's to the foster moms, the adoptive moms, the grandmothers, the aunts, the older sisters, the close friends and the complete strangers who take care of children who biologically aren't theirs and love them unconditionally.

thank you for making this world a better place.

here's to the motherless on mother's day.

open letter number nine

Mom,

i look back on baby pictures of myself,
you used to dress me up like a doll
i swear that's where i get my fashion sense from

everyone tells me all you ever wanted was to be a mom,
everyone tells me how you did such a good job
so, what happened? what changed?

you were just about my age when you had me,
i can't imagine having a child this early in life
do you think that having me at nineteen was a mistake?

did a switch in your head flip one day,
is that what made you walk away?

i know that mentally you aren't sane,
but these are the questions that i can't help but wonder
what happened?
what changed?

open letter number ten

Mom,

I don't think I was ever honest with you
about the embarrassment you caused me growing up

When I was thirteen and we moved in with dad
because you stopped taking care of us
kids in school used to ask me if you were on drugs

Ironically, dad was the one who wound up
self-medicating
with alcohol and cocaine

But,
nobody understood why or how a mother
could abandon her children out of nowhere

It was so hard to explain
what was going on

How do you tell someone that
your mother believes
that this is all God?

At that age, I didn't realize that
I didn't owe anyone an explanation

But now, here I am,
writing a book about it all
and owning
every embarrassing moment
that took place

Mom,

I was late to school almost every day
during my senior year of high school
did you know that?

I was late, almost every day,
because I had to drop Justin
off at school every morning

I'm not really sure what you were doing on those mornings
all I know is that you weren't around
and I was forced to pick up your slack

Not only did I drop him off every morning,
but I picked him up every afternoon

I always felt so strange as a seventeen-year-old girl,
sitting in the car,
waiting on the pick-up line
with middle-aged mothers in their minivans

I always wondered what people thought of me
when they saw me waiting there for Justin
I would get so worried that they thought I was a teen mom
and I wasn't wrong for thinking that way

Sometimes people would assume we were mother and son
and sometimes I would correct them
but, sometimes I would just go along with it
because it was just too weird to explain

I was really the only mother he knew at that time, anyway

03/17/2015

I'll never forget this day. It was the St. Patrick's day during my junior year of high school. After school, I needed to stop at the store to get something. I don't remember what I needed to buy, but that's unimportant. I never really shopped at Walmart. But, for some reason, I went there that day.

I walked into the store, and began browsing through the aisles. When, all of a sudden, I see my mother standing there. Right in one of the aisles. I didn't know what to do. So I just froze. I pretended that I didn't see her and tried to avoid this extremely awkward situation. I hadn't seen my mother in months at this time. But, she saw me.

She came over to me as if I was an old friend and started talking to me, asking how I was. She was dressed in a green shirt and wearing green eyeshadow for St. Patrick's Day. And, I just remember thinking, what the f*ck is going on right now? Why am I running into my MOM at the store randomly? What is she doing at Walmart right now? *Why is my life so weird?*

open letter number twelve

Mom,

I blocked you on social media.
I'm sorry.

I was just sick of you watching my Instagram stories,
when you don't hear any of my stories in real life.

I was just sick of you seeing my selfies,
when you don't see my face in person anymore.

I'm sorry.
But it just felt too weird to me.

I don't know why I'm sorry though.
Because you blocked your mother on social media, too.

That's one thing you and I have in common, I guess.

open letter number thirteen

Mom,

Since I was fifteen, it was my dream
to work in the fashion industry.
I didn't really care about much in high school
unless it had to do with what I was wearing.

Fashion was my first love.
I didn't care much about having a boyfriend
or going out on the weekends in high school.
I didn't use those things as a way to distract myself.
I used fashion.

It was a way for me to express myself,
before I knew how to express myself with words.
I spent hours every night before school,
trying on outfits, picking out accessories and shoes.
I read fashion books, I watched fashion movies,
I took fashion classes in school.

It was my escape.

A career in fashion was all I ever dreamed about.
I thought that it was what I wanted.

After being wait-listed by my dream school *(which completely crushed me)* and after skipping my first semester of college,
I finally got into the Fashion Institute of Technology.

I finally started living,
what I thought then,
was my dream.

But then, life happened.

After dad took his own life,
everything that happened made me change my mind.

Everything that happened made me feel like
I could be doing more for the world.

After three semesters of hard work,
I dropped out of my dream school like it was nothing.

I gave up on my fifteen-year-old self's goals.
I left all of my aspirations behind.

Now, I study psychology
to figure out what went wrong with your life.
Now, I study psychology
to figure out what went wrong with dad's life.
Now, I study psychology
so I can help kids who are in the same situation as I once was.

You may think that your absence hasn't affected me all that much.

But, actually, it was a domino effect that made me change
my perspective,
my college major,
and my career goals.

I don't know if this is a good or a bad thing.

But I do know that
I'm going to help a lot of people along the way.
And that's all that matters.

May 1st, 2018

To Whom It May Concern:

I wish to be released from my Spring 2018/Fall 2019 housing contract because I will be taking a semester or two off from college to mourn my father who I tragically lost to suicide just seven months ago on October 3rd, 2017. After his death, I didn't take any time off at all, and I pushed myself through the rest of the Fall 2017 semester as well as this current Spring 2018 semester. I thought that I would be fine because I was keeping my mind busy. However, doing this and pushing myself so hard has really affected my mental health and I haven't been able to keep up with my studies. I've been very depressed and filled with anxiety, and this has affected my ability to focus, along with my grades. I failed a class for the first time in my college career, and had to withdraw from it. So, as you can tell, I lost a lot of motivation. In addition, I have been very unhappy living away from my family during this time of loss. So, with that being said, I've decided that it would be best for myself to take some time off in order to focus on my mental health. Since I won't be attending school next semester and possibly the semester after that, I have no choice but to withdraw from my housing contract for Spring 2018/Fall 2019. I currently live in Kaufman Hall, and I will be vacating my dorm on May 21st, 2018. I hope that you can understand my reasoning for canceling my housing contract. My father's certificate of death is attached below. Feel free to contact me if you have any questions about this matter or need any further documentation. Thank you for understanding.

Best regards,

Jacquelyn Monserrat

To anyone thinking about taking time off from college:

- to focus on your mental health
- to mourn a loved one
- to work and save money
- to follow your dreams
- to figure out what you want to do with your life
- (add your own reason here)

Here is my advice: *Do it.*

Mom,

I was going through my Google Drive files and I found this.
This is the introduction paragraph of my admissions essay to the
Fashion Institute of Technology.

"Back in the sixth grade as I sat in computer class, my teacher said:
"Raise your hand if you are going to college." I looked around in
confusion as everyone in my class raised their hand, while I didn't.
College sounded like a foreign country to my 12-year-old self. I had
no idea what college I wanted to go to or what career I wanted
to pursue; it was the last thing on my mind. I've never been the
smartest, and the fact that I'm both athletically and musically im-
paired, didn't help. Nevertheless, I've always been that girl with an
impressionable sense of style. Fashion is not only something that
I am passionate about, but it has helped me get through hardships
and overcome insecurities. Personal style is a form of self-expres-
sion that allows me to be both creative and innovative on a daily
basis. However, not once did it ever cross my mind that I could make
a career out of this passion."

What a shame.

What a shame, that twelve-year-old me was the only one in an
entire classroom of sixth-graders who had no idea about college.

What a shame, that you weren't a role model for me. The fact that
you didn't make anything of yourself is on you. But, you could've
at least pushed your daughter to go further in life than you did.

What a shame, that you and dad used to tell me I needed to *just
find a rich husband* one day.

What a shame, that instead of telling me to become
a lawyer or a doctor myself, you and dad told me I should
make sure I marry one.

What a shame, that I thought I had no other skills
aside from dressing myself in stylish clothing.

What a shame, that I wrote the words
"I've never been the smartest." about myself,
all because I was never called smart growing up.

I was called *beautiful.*
I was called *skinny.*

And while it's important to compliment teenage girls on
their beauty, it's just as necessary to acknowledge their brains.

I was raised in such a way that made me believe that
my appearance on the outside defined who I am as a female.

Please.
Tell your daughters
they are smart
as often as you tell them
they are beautiful.

open letter number fifteen

Mom,

You weren't there
throughout my high school years

You weren't there
to check my report cards,
to sign my permission slips

You weren't there
when I got wait-listed
to my dream college
and cried my eyes out

You weren't there
when I got my first job
when I got my first paycheck

You weren't there
when I finally got
accepted into my dream college

You weren't there
to help me
move into my dorm

You weren't there
when I wrote
my first poetry book

You weren't there
to read it
to tell me what you think

You weren't there
to talk to me
when I decided to
leave my dream college

You weren't there
when I decided to
go back to college

You weren't there
when I decided to
change my major

You aren't here now
to experience
my journey with me

You aren't here now
to experience
all four of our
journeys with us

You've missed
dance recitals,
football games,
basketball games,
art shows,
graduations,
and so much more

You are going to miss all of this
three more times
if you don't come back into our lives

Hi how are you? I see you started a new college, I'm so proud of you. I also wanted to say you may not understand all you're and we're going through right now, but one day you will. You are my first beautiful daughter and nothing will ever change that, and God will restore us all in His perfect timing. I love you so and I always miss you everyday. Daddy is always watching out for you also.

- a text message from my mother after not hearing from her in over a year, February 8th, 2019, 4:29 PM

a general message

Stop asking kids
who have an estranged parent
where the parent is,
if they've seen the parent,
or if they've heard from the parent.

Nine times out of ten:
the answer is, no.

Ten times out of ten:
it hurts,
it's awkward,
and
we don't want to talk about them.

Please be more understanding.

Mom,

I'm just gonna take a moment to rant about
the fact that I had to take on your role growing up.

I was a teenager.

Teenagers are supposed to have chores, not be housewives.

I'm gonna say that again.

**Teenagers
are supposed to
have chores,
not be housewives.**

I spent my days
cleaning, cooking, doing laundry,
and driving *(your)* kids around,
while I was in high school and working a job of my own.

What were you doing during all of those times?

Everyone used to call me Cinderella as a joke,
Because I had to take on my mother's role.

I was fifteen.

And I was forced to

clean the house,

cook dinner,

do the dishes,

do everyone's laundry,

watch the kids,

take care of the dogs,

go grocery shopping,

run errands,

and eventually, pay bills, too.

There is a huge difference between
having chores and responsibilities as a teenager
and having to pick up your mother's slack.

They called me Cinderella
but there was no Fairy Godmother there to save me.

I was forced to save myself.

I will never forget
being twelve-years-old
and saying, *"Mom, I don't know how to"*
when she asked me to do the dishes
for the first time

She never taught me how to do anything
she didn't teach me how to clean, how to cook
and then all of a sudden
she expected me to do it all

Even before we didn't live with her anymore

She just stopped
being a mom

And expected me
to take on her role
without
preparing me
at all

After years of teaching me
nothing

She demanded of me,

"Go get your brothers
and sister
from the bus stop"

"Do the dishes"

"Do the laundry"

and sometimes, even

"Cook dinner"

while she sat on the couch

and watched TV shows
and YouTube videos

of *"pastors"*
telling her that

God was going to
giving her her breakthrough

if she sent them $500

i was only a child
i did not understand
what was happening to my mother
or why it was happening

i was confused
i was alone
i was embarrassed

but i was the oldest sibling
so the burden fell on me

and my siblings were
even younger
even more confused
even more alone
even more embarrassed

we were only children then
how were we supposed to understand?

but, the fact that we were children
and did not understand
is not a problem

i'm sure most people would agree

the problem
is that
so many adults
did not understand

so many adults
called my mother crazy

so many adults
called my mother lazy

all because her illness was invisible to them

all because they couldn't see her pain with their eyes

- if she had a physical illness, would you all have said the same?

open letter number seventeen

Mom,

I just opened up the Facebook app on my phone
and saw a post that said,
"I am a strong woman because a strong woman raised me."

A bunch of girls were re-posting it
and tagging their mothers in it.

Seeing posts like these truly *stings.*

There are no other words to describe
how it feels other than
complete and utter emptiness.

Here's to the girls who
don't have a mother to tag in Facebook posts.

Here's to the girls who
have no idea what a true mother-daughter bond is like.

Here's to the girls who
are strong because they *didn't* have a strong woman to raise them.

- We are the strongest.

"But…
you'll be a great mother one day
since your mother wasn't around."

- Thanks, but telling me this doesn't make anything better. At all.

Growing up, I thought I was the only one in the world who
had an *absent mother.*

Growing up, I thought I was the only one in the world who
had a *mentally ill mother.*

Growing up, I thought I was the only one in the world who
had an *unstable mother.*

It was not until I was out of high school that I realized,
there were so many others going through the same thing as me.

We all suffered in silence.
We all thought we were the only ones.
We all had no idea how similar our lives were.

Imagine how much we could've helped one another,
if the stigma around having an absent mother didn't exist.

Imagine how much we could've helped one another,
if we felt more comfortable
talking about our situations without being judged.

It is time to open up
and help one another heal
from our motherless upbringings.

People always assume,
"So, since your mom isn't in your life,
she must not be a pleasant person to be around..."
And I always reply with,
"Actually, no, my mother wouldn't hurt a fly."

No matter how much my mother has hurt me,
she is still one of the kindest people I've ever known.
It's so strange, I know.

She is not evil, manipulative, or mean-spirited in any way.
She was not even a bad mother when she was around.

She is *mentally ill.*
I don't even think she realizes the hurt she has caused.

If only she had the right people in her life to lead her to help. If
only the people in her life didn't brainwash her. *This could've all
been avoided.* This domino effect of unfortunate events would've
never happened.

My mother would've gotten help. She would've continued to work
and get on her own two feet. She would've *never* left us.

My siblings and I would've never had to move in with our father
full-time. He wouldn't have developed an addiction from all of the
stress. And ultimately, he wouldn't have taken his own life.

Things are not supposed to be this way.
They were *never* supposed to be this way.

If it wasn't for my mother being brainwashed, life would be a lot
different. My siblings and I wouldn't be growing up without one
another. We wouldn't be living in four different places right now.
That has to be the saddest part of it all.

my mother
is not
a monster

she doesn't have
one mean bone
in her body

she is an angel

she has a
heart of gold

she is a rose
without any thorns

- yet, somehow, she still hurt me.

sometimes
i wish that
my mother
had a
physical disability
instead of
a mental one

at least then,
she wouldn't have to
suffer in silence

at least then,
she wouldn't have to
deal with people who
don't understand her

at least then,
her illness wouldn't be
completely invisible

if my mother was
in a wheelchair
people would understand
her inability to take care of her kids

the problem is
there is no
handicap sign
for your mind

open letter number eighteen

Mom,

Do you even know anything about me?

You don't know what my apartment looks like,
or what kind of car I drive

You don't know about the TV shows that make me laugh,
or the songs that make me cry

You don't know how horrible I am at math,
or how often I get my hair dyed

You don't know that I don't eat meat anymore,
or how I like to put hot sauce on everything

You don't know about the friends I've grown apart from,
or about the new ones I've made

You don't know what size jeans I wear,
or my favorite lipstick shade

A mother is supposed to know these things,
I don't really know what else to say

Maybe you would know these things
if you hadn't walked away

All of my childhood memories were left behind.

I don't have the notebooks I used to write in,
the scrapbooks I used to make.
I don't have anything.

Do you even know that, Mom?

Do you even realize the damage that's been done?

It's ironic, because I don't remember
much of my childhood,
anyway.

So, maybe it's better that everything was left behind.

Maybe it's better that I don't have
those old notebooks I used to write in.

you can't just be a part-time mom
this is not a part-time job

this is a commitment for life
whether or not you're someone's wife

you can't just give up on your kids
and expect them to easily move on and live

we are all messed up in our own ways
because you weren't there for our childhood days

mother dearest
i want you to hear this
mother dearest
i want you to feel this
mother dearest
i want you to see this
mother dearest
i want you to know
what your absence
has done to us all

i starved myself for years
to cope with the pain
i obsessed with my image and my size
to hide the pain i was feeling inside

larissa cut her wrists
just to try to feel something, anything
she was crying out for help
and you weren't there to hear her

paulie seemed to deal with your absence the healthiest
he went to the gym and played sports
to get his thoughts away from you
but he had a lot of unexpressed emotions that he held inside
for a long, long time

justin was the youngest, justin was the baby
he didn't understand why you weren't there
he had big, big feelings that he didn't know how to express
so he expressed them in anger, he express them in tears
and you weren't there to console him throughout the years

mother dearest
i just want you to hear this
mother dearest
i just want you to know

my mother is not a narcissist
my mother was never abusive
she is simply absent from my life

that is my mother wound

but, so many others have a mother wound that is much different

so many others deal with a
toxic, narcissistic, verbally abusive mother every day

so many others deal with a
mother who is around, but might as well not be

so many others deal with a
mother who they argue with every single day

so many others deal with a
mother who kills their spirit with her words

so many others probably *wish*
their mother wasn't around

so many others probably *wish*
they had my *mother wound* instead

yet sometimes, i wish that i had theirs,
because at least then,
my mother would be in my life

there is such an irony in it all

We all have different mother wounds,
               and they are all valid.
Some of us have
        an absent mother.

Some of us have
        a mentally-ill mother.

Some of us have
        an abusive mother.

Some of us have
        a narcissistic mother.

Some of us have
        an alcoholic mother.

Some of us have
        a drug-addicted mother.

Some of our mothers are in our lives
           and some are not.

Some of us are foster children
           and some of us were adopted.

We all have different mother wounds,
          but we all have one thing in common.

We're all trying to figure out
        the same *why.*

We're all just trying to understand
          why our mother rejected us
              in one way or another.

People often tell me that I look like my mother.

They say that I have her
pretty green eyes
and her nice, thick hair.

I mean, she is my mother, right?

I remember looking at a photo of her as a teenager, and saying
"I don't remember taking this picture."

And my aunt telling me,
"No, that's your mom when she was your age."

So, maybe I do look like her.
But I don't see it.
I don't see what they see.

Maybe it's because
I can't recall the last time I've seen her face.

Maybe it's because
I'm so detached.

Maybe it's hard to admit
that you look so much like someone
who hurt you so bad.

Or maybe it's because
I'm so afraid of winding up like her one day.

This is not the kind of trauma you can see with your eyes.
No, this kind of trauma is invisible.
It lives deep inside.

The worst thing about it is it doesn't go away.
Bruises heal, scars fade.
But abandonment issues stay.

They eat away at my soul every day.
I don't get to hide them with makeup and band-aids.
These issues come with me wherever I go.

But, nobody can see them.
They're buried deep inside my bones.
They're scars on my heart that go untold.

So this is me starting the healing process,
because I can't go on living this way.

This trauma needs to heal so I can start a new day.

chapter three
the breakthrough

my mother has been waiting for
her breakthrough for years

ironically,
this chapter
is titled *breakthrough*
but no, it is not
about her breakthrough

this chapter is about
her children's breakthrough

it is about our healing, our recovery

it is about how we survived
all of these years
of our mother
sitting around
waiting for her *breakthrough*

It's not that I don't believe in God,
it's that I don't believe in my mother's God

The God that told her
to stop working

The God that told her
it was okay to stop working

The God that told her
to abandon her children

The God that keeps telling her
it's okay to stay away from her children

The God that told her
to stop showing up for life

The God that told her
it's okay to stop showing up for life

The God that told her that she'd get her *breakthrough*
The God that keeps telling her that she'll get her *breakthrough*

It's been eight years.
When exactly is this breakthrough supposed to happen?

To the kids whose moms are alive, but aren't in their lives:

You are not alone.
I know it feels like you are the only person in the universe who
doesn't have a mother in their life, but honey, I was you. I am you.

I've heard the words *"I'm sorry to ask you this, but is your mother
dead? You never seem to talk about her,"* too many times to count.

I went to doctor's appointments with grandparents, aunts,
and uncles, while my mother was nowhere to be found.

I shook my head *yes* when teacher's asked *"did you get your
mother to sign this permission slip?"* Meanwhile, I hadn't seen my
mother's face in over a month.

I went to friend's houses and watched them take their mothers for
granted, while I grew up without one.

I was raised by everyone *but* my mother.

But mostly, I was raised by myself.

I was you. *I am you.* You are not the only one.

august 11th, 2018— a journal entry

It's my 20th birthday.

But it doesn't feel like my 20th birthday.

In fact, it doesn't feel like a birthday at all.
Maybe it will in the morning.
Who knows. It's 2:39am right now.

I guess I don't think about it enough but it's hard to celebrate life
when one of your parents ended their own.

How ironic is it?
A person who gave life
to four human beings
took their own.

Isn't that… *something?*

Anyway—at the same time, I am happy
because I can appreciate life so much more now.

But it still pains me to think that so many others out there want to
end their own lives while I am celebrating mine today. If only they
know how worth it they are.

But, all in all, I am happy to be alive.
Life is something to be celebrated.
Not just on birthdays, but every day.

So, happy 20th birthday to me.

sunday, august 11th, 2019

Happy 21st Birthday I love you love you love you

- A surprising text from my mother, who I didn't hear from on my previous two birthdays

To the kids who can relate to the words in this book:

I am here to tell you that there is light
that comes after the darkness.

There are rainbows
that come after the rain.

There is laughter
that comes after the pain.

There are so many
good days ahead.

If I could go through all that I did
and still stand tall.

If I could go through all that I did
and still be here.

If I could go through all that I did
and still live.

There is no reason why you can't, too.

Going through a lot makes you a very laid-back person.
It makes you put a lot of things into a new perspective.

I used to be so up-tight.
I used to let the little things stress me out.
I couldn't sleep if my room was a mess.

Now, I sleep peacefully with
piles of clothing on my bedroom floor.

I used to obsess over my appearance.
I'd spend hours in front of the mirror
making sure my make-up looked perfect.

Now, I get ready in under thirty minutes.
I still wear make-up,
but I don't care if it looks perfect.

I used to freak out if
one of my belongings got ruined.

Now, I don't care
even if I catch my dog chewing one of my shoes.

Going through things makes you realize that
there are bigger problems in this world.

To spend our lives
worrying about the little things
is to waste our lives.

A messy room can always be cleaned.
Make-up washes off, anyway.
And our belongings are replaceable.
But, life isn't.

a realization
my trauma is something that happened to me.
it does not define me.

My trauma does not define me.
I used to think that it did.
But, then I realized,

I am not
"the girl who had a rough life."

I am not
"the girl with an absent mother."

I am not
"the girl whose father killed himself."

I am not
"the girl who was abused and neglected."

I am not
"the girl who had to grow up too fast."

None of this defines me.
None of this defines my future.

The only person who can define me, is *me.*

Growing up without a mother
is something
that I will be recovering from
for the rest of
my life.

What does recovery look like?

Recovery looks like
chewed up fingernails and overgrown toenails
dressed up in three-week-old chipped nail polish.

Recovery looks like
an unmade bed and baskets of unfolded clean laundry that
probably won't make it into the dresser drawers until next week.

Recovery looks like
greasy hair and empty bottles of dry shampoo
lined up on the bathroom counter.

Recovery looks like unshaved legs in the summer.

Recovery looks like falling asleep without
washing your face, and having no shame about it.

Recovery looks like staying up until four o'clock in the morning
and sleeping until two o'clock in the afternoon.

Recovery looks like acne. A lot of it.

Recovery looks like things are getting worse.

But, things often get worse before they get better.

- *Beautiful plants cannot grow without a little bit of dirt.*

Are you okay?
Yeah, I'm okay. If okay means not sleeping at night because I'm afraid of my own dreams.

Are you okay?
Yeah, I'm okay. If okay means sleeping all day because I don't sleep at night and well, I need to sleep at some point.

Are you okay?
Yeah, I'm okay. If okay means feeling proud of myself because I'm not afraid to walk down the street without pepper spray anymore.

Are you okay?
Yeah, I'm okay. If okay means crying because I gained ten pounds, but not having the motivation to do anything about it.

Are you okay?
Yeah, I'm okay. If okay means I either eat too much or I don't have an appetite at all.

Are you okay?
Yeah, I'm okay. If okay means canceling plans because I don't have the energy to take a shower.

Are you okay?
Yeah, I'm okay. If okay means not having the energy to get out of the shower once I'm in it, either.

Are you okay?
Yeah, I'm okay. If okay means I couldn't finish my associate's degree because it was too overwhelming.

Are you okay?
Yeah, I'm okay. If okay means wanting to buy a one-way plane ticket, fly across the country and escape.

Are you okay?

Yeah, I'm okay.

I'm just tired.

Really. Really. *Tired.*

My dad has been dead for over two years.
And I haven't seen my mom in over two years.
Sometimes I feel like she's dead, too.

They say that the five stages of grief are:

Denial

      Anger

            Bargaining

                  Depression

                      &

                          Acceptance

And I really don't know if I experienced these all at once,
or none at all.

- I'm still healing, and that's okay.

to the kids who are mourning parents:

it's okay to feel however you need to feel.

cry. scream. cry some more.

be angry. be mad at the world. be frustrated.

or, don't cry. don't scream.

be happy. be hopeful. be positive.

feel however you need to feel.

take your time to grieve.

don't rush the process.

take things day by day. minute by minute. second by second.

let others be there for you.
cry on your friend's shoulders.
hold your loved ones tight.

you don't always have to be so strong.
it's okay to be needy.
it's okay to be weak.

take time off from work and school to be with your family.
or, don't.
go back right away and keep yourself busy.

do whatever works for you.

please, don't *ever* let anyone tell you how to grieve,
because we all grieve differently.

Choosing to be kind in a world that hasn't
been so kind to me,
is the strongest thing I've ever done.

My problem is
I understand *too much.*

I understand that he has anger issues
because of his father.

I understand that she has anxiety
because of her mother.

I understand that people become who they are
because of their upbringing.

She seeks attention from others because
her parents never showed her attention.

He hides his feelings because
he wasn't ever allowed to
express them growing up.

The truth is we all have issues from our childhood.

It's time to start being more *understanding* of one another.
It's time to start being more *kind* to one another.

For most people, texting their mom is a normal activity. For others, it is an *act of bravery.*

hi mom i'm sorry we haven't talked in a while. i hope you're doing well. aunt nene is really sad because today is national siblings day and she misses you and uncle adam. also she has been really sick. i think it would make her happy if you texted her even just to say hi.

- an act of bravery, 4/10/20, 4:06 pm

dear younger me,

breathe in // breathe out // breathe in // breathe out

you're going to be okay

dear younger me,

please do not grow resentful
please do not grow hateful

please do not let
your pretty little mind
be full of
negative thoughts

i know it's hard
i know, i do

but you, my darling, you
are going to be good

you will have a life of
laughter
and fun
and peace

you will learn to understand
what led to all of this happening

you may never understand *why*
but you will understand *how*

i know it's hard not to worry

but, i am telling you
you will be okay
you will be okay
you will be okay

a realization II
being traumatized at a young age isn't
what made me strong.
i never needed those experiences to be strong.
i was already strong.
that's how i survived.

to the kids who grew up motherless
please understand this

we didn't need those experiences
to become stronger

we didn't need those experiences
to learn disappointment

we needed to be taken care of
we needed our mother
and she wasn't there

our strength did not come from our pain
we were already strong
how do you think we survived?

we're all just trying to express ourselves

we're all just trying to fill a void

we're all just trying to feel full in such an empty world

some of us write poetry

some of us sing and play guitar

some of us tattoo our bodies

some of us dye our hair different colors

we all cling to what helps us express ourselves

we all cling to what fills the void

we all cling to what makes us feel *full* in this

empty, empty world

in order to heal, we need to let go
of anything, of anyone
that is costing us our peace of mind

unfollow the person on social media
who keeps posting about drama and nonsense

block the phone number
of that ex you can't stop texting

quit the job
where you're being mistreated by your boss

drop the class that
you're failing because the professor is horrible

get rid of anything that
is causing you anxiety in your life

even if that means
letting go
of your own
toxic family

in order to heal,
this is what
we need to do

nothing is worth
our peace,
our clarity,
our sanity

open letter number nineteen

Mom,

If I die,
technically,
you are my next of kin.

And if you die,
technically,
I am your next of kin.

When it comes to our blood,
we are the closest.

But, when it comes to our bond,
we are the farthest apart.

- a sad realization.

open letter number twenty

Mom,

It is April 19th, 2020 at 2:34 AM.

We've been in the midst of the COVID-19 pandemic for about a
month now. Going outside is scary and anxiety-provoking.

And I can't stop thinking about you.

I can't stop thinking about the fact that you feel this way
every
single
day.

You live your life in *isolation.*

Your life is a constant *quarantine.*

I can't stop thinking about how crippling
it must be to fear everyday life.

It's only been about a month that I've been experiencing being
afraid to go outside, to go in public, to be around other people.

It's only been a month and my mental health is terrible.
I am sad,
I cry for no reason,
and I can't seem to pull myself out of it.

But, you have been going through this for
just about eight years now.

I'm so sorry that you live your life
feeling this way, Mom. *I'm so, so sorry.*

Mom,

You shouldn't be ashamed
to have depression
You shouldn't be ashamed
to have anxiety
You shouldn't be ashamed
to not have the motivation to get out of bed every day

Mental illness is real,
mental illness is valid

You have a chemical imbalance in your brain
and that is nothing to be ashamed of

However,
You *should be* ashamed that you let your children suffer
You *should be* ashamed that you refuse to get treatment
You *should be* ashamed that you won't admit you need help

That is the problem here
The problem is *not* your illness
The problem is your lack of self-awareness

The problem is
that you've been going untreated for years
The problem is
that your mental illness has taken over your life
The problem is
that you haven't even *tried* to get better

I know it's hard,
but, you just can't
live your life like this forever

Mom,

how ironic is it that
your mental breakdown
is what caused us to
move in with dad

and then,
us moving in with dad
is what caused
dad's mental breakdown?

my dad ended his life
by hanging himself

my mother ended her life
by giving up on herself

i can't lie and say that
i don't worry about
getting a call one day
that my mother took her own life, too

this is something that
lingers on my mind often

i don't think i could bare the thought
of losing both of my parents to suicide

but then again,
we lost her so long ago

she is breathing,
but is she really alive?

is it still considered a life
if you are not living it?

the night my dad killed himself,
my mom was with us

after getting a call from my uncle
while sitting in my college dorm

i packed a bag in a hurry
i was shaking
i was sad
i was angry
i was confused

i got a ride home
to long island
from new york city

and i came home
to my sister in tears
and my mother consoling her

my mother said
for years
that she was afraid
of our father

she said for years
that she stayed away
because of him

and she had every reason
to be afraid

we thought that she would come around
we thought that she would want to be around
and, we wanted her around

we enjoyed having the comfort of our mother for once

but no,
she only
came around
once or twice
after that night

the last time we saw her
was on december 25th, 2017
yes, the last time we saw her
was on christmas day

and then,
she went
back into hiding

her kids
lost their father
to suicide

and
she still
does not
come around

open letter number twenty three

Mom,

It's Christmas day.
And it's been 365 days since I've last seen your face.

The sound of your voice is a sheer echo in my brain.
The color of your eyes has faded from my memory.

Do you remember the sound of my voice?
Do you remember the color of my eyes?

You and I were once one,
how are we now divided?

You missed an entire year of my life.
And I'll never understand why.

Why did you leave us right after Christmas day?
Why did you bring us presents,
and then deprive us of your presence?

Is it because you resent us?
Is it because you can't handle us?

No matter what the reason is,
I just hope that you're okay.

But please don't tell me that the reason you left is God
Because He showed me that it wasn't supposed to be this way.

- written on December 25th, 2018.

open letter number twenty four

Mom,

About a year ago, I was diagnosed with Endometriosis.

Aunt Janine had it when she was my age, too.

Thank God I have her,
because I didn't even know what it was
until she told me about it.

God has a funny way of working things out. She has been with me
through all of the pain, and she knows everything. *But you don't.*

So, if you ever read this, I just thought you should know.

My period was irregular for months.
My body was constantly bloated and in so much pain.
The doctor prescribed me birth control pills to ease the symptoms.

Also, I have a huge cyst on my left ovary that the doctor is hoping
will shrink after taking birth control for a while. The pills help, but
the week of my period, I still feel like I'm dying.

I just thought you should know.

Also.
Endometriosis can cause infertility.
Which is extremely ironic.

Because raising my younger siblings
caused me to grow up saying I never wanted to have kids.
Be careful what you wish for, right?

"I have to be honest, I got really jealous
when you all started getting closer with
aunt nene.

I got really jealous when you all
started calling her your Mom,"
my mother told me one day.

Yet, her sister being a mom to me
is the first time
I had any normalcy in a parent figure.
And this didn't happen until I was nineteen.

Yet, if she was a mom to me,
she wouldn't have to feel any jealousy.

Giving birth to me
and giving me my name
does not make you my mom.

Being a mom
means
being around.

Being a mom
means
having memories.

Being a mom
means
being there
through all the ups and downs.

You are not here, Mom,
but your sister is.

things didn't have to be this way

your sister didn't have to become our mom

things didn't have to be this way

my sister didn't have to move in with your mom

things didn't have to be this way

your kids didn't have to be scattered

things didn't have to be this way

mom, we could've had better days

a realization III
my parent's mistakes are their mistakes.
not mine.

my	parent's	mistakes	are	not	my	mistakes.
my	parent's	mistakes	are	not	my	mistakes.
my	parent's	mistakes	are	not	my	mistakes.
my	parent's	mistakes	are	not	my	mistakes.
my	parent's	mistakes	are	not	my	mistakes.
my	parent's	mistakes	are	not	my	mistakes.
my	parent's	mistakes	are	not	my	mistakes.
my	parent's	mistakes	are	not	my	mistakes.
my	parent's	mistakes	are	not	my	mistakes.
my	parent's	mistakes	are	not	my	mistakes.
my	parent's	mistakes	are	not	my	mistakes.
my	parent's	mistakes	are	not	my	mistakes.
my	parent's	mistakes	are	not	my	mistakes.
my	parent's	mistakes	are	not	my	mistakes.
my	parent's	mistakes	are	not	my	mistakes.
my	parent's	mistakes	are	not	my	mistakes
my	parent's	mistakes	are	not	my	mistakes.
my	parent's	mistakes	are	not	my	mistakes.
my	parent's	mistakes	are	not	my	mistakes.
my	parent's	mistakes	are	not	my	mistakes.
my	parent's	mistakes	are	not	my	mistakes.
my	parent's	mistakes	are	not	my	mistakes.
my	parent's	mistakes	are	not	my	mistakes.
my	parent's	mistakes	are	not	my	mistakes.
my	parent's	mistakes	are	not	my	mistakes.
my	parent's	mistakes	are	not	my	mistakes.
my	parent's	mistakes	are	not	my	mistakes.
my	parent's	mistakes	are	not	my	mistakes.
my	parent's	mistakes	are	not	my	mistakes.
my	parent's	mistakes	are	not	my	mistakes.

Mom,

Two of your four kids
were able to seek psychological help.

Two of your four kids
stayed in an inpatient hospital to better their mental health.

Two of your four kids
are taking medication to better their mental health.

Two of your four kids
were able to learn that it's okay to ask for help.

Two of your four kids
are doing so much better because they accepted help.

Why can't you?

Mom,

All of your four kids
were able to find healthy coping skills.

All of your four kids
are able to go on in life despite their trauma.

All of your four kids
were able to overcome their anxiety and depression.

All of your four kids
were able to turn what we went through into our motivation.

All of your four kids
had their breakthrough.

Why can't you?

Mom,

Here is an update on your children.

I'm twenty-one now and I'll be twenty-two soon. I live in a cute little apartment with my boyfriend, Chris, who you never met. I pay rent. I pay for my own car that I own. I'm completely financially independent. And I'm proud of myself, because most people my age aren't. I go to college on Tuesday's and Thursday's and I work as a waitress most of the other days. I mean, we're in the middle of a pandemic, so right now, I'm mostly just at home. But when life is normal, that's what my life consists of. I don't go out often. I like to be a homebody. I love doing simple things like getting coffee, going to farmer's markets, and shopping at thrift stores. My life is simple and peaceful. And I love it.

I am so proud of myself, and you should be, too.

Paulie is eighteen now. He's graduating high school soon. But, sadly, his class probably won't have a graduation ceremony because of the pandemic. So, I guess you don't have to worry about not being there for it. Paulie spends most of his time working out and training for football. That's always been his therapy. He always eats healthy, he loves music, and he still loves to draw like he did when he was a kid. He's starting college soon and will continue to play football in college, too. He's always been mature for his age, but now, more than ever, he has grown and matured so much. He went through a rough patch in the beginning of 2020, but he came out of it better, stronger, and wiser.

I am so proud of him, and you should be, too.

Larissa is sixteen now. She's all the way in Florida with grandma. And we miss her a lot. It's so strange growing up scattered all over the place. But, her and I text and FaceTime constantly. We're closer now more than ever. I wish we were this close as sisters when we were younger. Larissa has overcome so much and she's doing an amazing job at life. She takes college classes at a college campus along with her online high school classes. She is probably going to graduate high school with an associate's degree. She is so smart and even more talented. She paints, she draws, and she writes poetry, too. She also teaches art classes to little kids at her church. After high school, she plans on going to college to become a psychiatric nurse. Larissa is an amazing girl with a huge heart.

I am so proud of her, and you should be, too.

Justin is fourteen now. I cannot believe how much he has grown. Justin is smarter than most people I know. He already thinks about running businesses and ways to make money at his young age. He is often on the honor roll at school and he gets the highest grades without even trying. Justin is one of the only students in his grade to get certified in Microsoft Excel, which is very hard to do. He is such a kind person with a big, big heart. If you ask him for help, he will jump up and help you right away. Just like Paulie and Larissa, Justin also enjoys drawing. He also loves playing basketball, too. I have no doubt that Justin will be amazingly successful in every area of his life, and I cannot wait to watch his path unfold.

I am so proud of him, and you should be, too.

growing up
motherless
does not mean that
you cannot
find the strength
to rise above it

my heart beats for
all of the kids
who grew up
motherless

thank you for reading . . .

a letter from me to you

dear reader,

you just read all of the emotions i've been afraid to express since the age of thirteen. you just read the truth the i've been afraid to face for years. you just read my heart and soul.

whether you were able to relate to my story or not, i hope that these words helped you heal in some way. i hope that these words brought you comfort.

for those of you who grew up motherless, i hope that this book showed you that you are not alone. i hope this book felt like a hug, or a cup of warm tea. i hope you know that i am here for you, always.

for those of you who didn't grow up motherless, i hope this book helped you understand what it was like for those of us who did. i hope that this book brings you a newfound appreciation for your own mothers.

we all have our own trauma. we all have our own pain. and we all have our own stories to tell. whether you had your mother in your life or not, your trauma and your pain are valid. you're allowed to feel all of your feelings.

if you have been wanting to write about your own pain, your own trauma, your own story, i encourage you to do so. put down this book and pick up a pen and paper. the world needs to hear all of our stories.

xoxo jacquelyn lee

about the author

jacquelyn lee is a twenty-one-year-old from new york. she is best known for her debut poetry book, *under the influence.* she wrote *mind over mother* as a sister book to *under the influence.* together, both of these books tell the story of jacquelyn's messy childhood. writing poetry books about her childhood was never something she thought she would do. it all just sort of happened. yet, it's one of the best things that have ever happened for her. writing poetry has helped her heal, learn, and grow in many ways.

currently, jacquelyn is attending stony brook university, where she is pursuing a bachelor's degree in psychology with a minor in writing. she aspires to become a mental health counselor in the future. however, she will never stop writing books. jacquelyn plans on spending her life helping others affected by abuse, trauma, addiction, and mental illness. overall, both her mission and passion in life is to advocate for mental health.

to stay connected with jacquelyn, and for updates on her upcoming books, you can find her as *@jacquelyn.lee.poetry* on instagram and as *@jacquelynpoetry* on twitter.

about the book

mind over mother
is for every child of
an estranged mother.

it is for every child of
a mentally ill mother.

it is for every child of
an emotionally unavailable mother.

it is for every child of
a religiously delusional mother.

mind over mother
is breakdown
breakaway
& breakthrough.

it is bringing awareness to
those who grew up motherless.

it is a collection of
poems,
essays,
&
open letters
to my estranged mother.

a final letter to my mother

Mom,

I'm not sure if you will ever read this book.
I'm not sure if it'll ever reach your hands.
I'm not sure if you even know that I'm writing this.

But, if you ever do happen to read this book,
I hope you get this far. I hope that this book can open your eyes.
I hope that this book can make you realize that you need help.

I hope that this book can make you realize that
there is no shame in needing help.

We are all human.
None of us are perfect.

Some people need to take insulin to treat their diabetes.
Some people need to get chemotherapy to treat their cancer.
You happen to need to get treatment for your mental illness.
And that is okay.

I hope you know I love you.
I hope you know I care about you.

I wrote this with the best intentions.
I wrote this with all of my heart and soul.

I hope you are able to recover.
I hope you are able to stop being afraid.
I hope you are able to live a full life one day.

From the one you gave life to,

Jacquelyn Lee

Made in the USA
Columbia, SC
14 June 2020

10842056R00087